To My
Beautiful,
Remarkable
Daughter

Edited by
Patricia Wayant

Blue Mountain Press™
Boulder, Colorado

We gratefully acknowledge the permission granted by the following authors, publishers, and authors' representatives to reprint poems or excerpts from their publications: Susan Polis Schutz for "I Love You Every Minute of Every Day, My Beautiful Daughter," "The mother-daughter relationship...," "To My Daughter, with Love, on the Important Things in Life," "Lean against a tree...," and "You are such a delight...." Copyright © 1986, 1987 by Stephen Schutz and Susan Polis Schutz. And for "This life is yours...." Copyright © 1979 by Continental Publications. All rights reserved. Erin McGraw for "You Are Everything I Ever Hoped for in a Daughter...." Copyright © 2010 by Erin McGraw. All rights reserved. Robert Sexton for "A Daughter's Gift." Copyright © 1995 by Robert Sexton. All rights reserved. Fisher King Press for "You know I love all my children..." from THE MOTHERLINE by Naomi Ruth Lowinsky, PhD. Copyright © 1992, 2009 by Naomi Ruth Lowinsky, PhD. All rights reserved. *The Huffington Post*, www.huffingtonpost.com, for "Our daughters will play..." from "Empowering Women Around the World" by Melinda Gates (*The Huffington Post*: April 11, 2007). Copyright © 2007 by Melinda Gates. All rights reserved. And for "My Letter to (unnamed)" by Naomi Wolf (*The Huffington Post*: April 20, 2007). Copyright © 2007 by Naomi Wolf. All rights reserved. Beyond Words Publishing, Hillsboro, Oregon, for "For me, having a daughter means..." from LIVE IN THE MOMENT by Julie Clark Robinson. Copyright © 2004 by Julie Clark Robinson. All rights reserved. April Aragam for "Daughters bring laughter and happiness...." Copyright © 2010 by April Aragam. All rights reserved.

Acknowledgments are continued on the last page.

Library of Congress Control Number: 2010903922
ISBN: 978-1-59842-524-6

Blue Mountain Arts, Inc.

P.O. Box 4549, Boulder, Colorado 80306

Contents

(Authors listed in order of first appearance)

To My Beautiful, Remarkable Daughter

I want you to know
how great it is to be
the parent of a daughter like you.

I want to tell you how proud I am
of all you've done and everything
you've become.

I want to say what a joy it was
to watch you grow up,
and what an amazing and
rewarding and loving experience
it continues to be.

Every time I see you, I know that
I am looking at as remarkable a gift
as anyone has ever been given.

And I know that I could have hoped
and prayed and dreamed all my life...
and I could have wished on a
million stars...

But I couldn't have been blessed with
   anyone more beautiful...
      than the daughter
      that you are.

                    ✿ Chris Gallatin

You Are Everything I Ever Hoped for in a Daughter... and More

I will never forget the way your tiny hand wrapped around my finger as you took your first cautious steps. I remember looking down at you and wondering... who would you be?

As you grew, with each accomplishment big or small, I looked at you with such pride and wondered who you would be someday. I realized I had to let you make your own mistakes and learn your lessons. All I could do was love you with my whole heart and let you know I would always be there for you.

Now, as we sit and talk, I realize your hand is no longer little — and neither are you. You have grown into a young woman who is loving, caring, intelligent, responsible, and happy. You have learned your lessons and grown from them, and you're making it in this world just fine.

I realize I no longer have to wonder who you are going to be... because you have turned out to be everything I dreamed you could be and more.

❀ Erin McGraw

I remember how before you were born, I hoped for a daughter. Little did I know then that what I was really hoping for was a friend — someone to laugh with even when life was not funny, someone whose very presence would fill me with a love so deep and pure that I could finally understand what it meant to actually love someone more than I loved myself.

Lea Walsh

*T*o have a daughter like you is
to feel proud when I wake up each day,
to feel peace in my heart,
to hear the music of joy and laughter
wherever I go,
and to walk with pride and happiness
in my heart for all we share.

Jacqueline Schiff

A Daughter's Gift

When I imagine
the life you will live,
I think of the pleasure
your presence will give;
I see the joy
your smile will light
and the wonders you'll weave
when your dreams take flight.
I feel the hope
that will grow with your grace
and the difference you'll make
to each heart you embrace.
I imagine your life
as I know it will be;
for, my daughter, you've given
all this to me.

Robert Sexton

There's Something Special About Having a Daughter

For me, having a daughter means that all of my wishes have been granted, and the rest of my dreams are up to me to fulfill. I'd like her to grow into my best friend. She doesn't have to be perfect. She just needs to exist. Because of her, my growing older seems like a good thing. I want to watch her become a mother... to help her make choices... to carry all that I hold dear into the world after I'm gone. Because of her, I am complete.

❀ Julie Clark Robinson

*O*ur daughters will play a crucial role in creating a world where everyone has the opportunity to live a healthy, productive life. We should be encouraging and nurturing them to do that work well.

❀ Melinda Gates

*O*ur daughters are the most precious of our treasures, the dearest possessions of our homes, and the objects of our most watchful love.

❀ Margaret E. Sangster

*Y*ou know I love all my children. But there is something very special about [my daughter]. It's as though all the good fairies were standing around her cradle when she was born and they just gave her everything. She is a life enhancer. She is a window into another world.

❀ Naomi Ruth Lowinsky, PhD

A daughter is a little piece
    of yourself
looking back at you.
She is another chance for you
    to realize the dreams
        of your past.
She is God's most precious gift,
    and adventures without end.

A daughter is your best creation.
She's a best friend
    and a fashion adviser.

Only she knows why
    you love purple
        and hate turnips.

A daughter is never-ending love,
    given and received,
and learning to love yourself.
Of all the things that
    happen in life,
        a daughter is the best.

❀ Brenda A. Morris

*D*aughters bring laughter
and happiness to the world
They make each day worth waking up for
The sun shines a little brighter
The flowers smell a little sweeter
Daughters teach us lessons
we would never learn otherwise
A daughter is the sister we never had
and the friend we always longed for
Daughters are our hope for the future

❀ April Aragam

A daughter improves your day just by being
a part of it and blesses your world — over
and over again — just by being in it.

❀ Elizabeth Rose

I Love You Every Minute of Every Day, My Beautiful Daughter

I looked at you today
and saw the same beautiful eyes
that looked at me with love
when you were a baby
I looked at you today
and saw the same beautiful mouth
that made me cry when you first smiled at me
when you were a baby
It was not long ago
that I held you in my arms
long after you fell asleep
and I just kept rocking you
all night long
I looked at you today
and saw my beautiful daughter
no longer a baby
but a beautiful person
with a full range of emotions
feelings, ideas and goals

Every day is exciting
as I continue to watch you grow
I want you to always know that
in good and in bad times
I will love you
and that no matter what you do
or how you think
or what you say
you can depend on
my support, guidance
friendship and love
every minute of every day

❀ Susan Polis Schutz

My Daughter in the Garden

One — two — three, she counts and drops
the seeds in shallow holes. *Bye-bye*,
she says. *See you soon!* Palms pat

the dampened soil. Hands clasp and twirl
a daisy stem. *One — two — three*, she counts
and plucks its tattered cape. *Bye-bye*, she calls

to each. Petals dip and scoop the air
in their narrow sails. *Away! Away!* A swallow
cries. Wings scissor the ragged sky. An aircraft

roars. Sound fills my chest and drains away.
One — two — three, I count the years. Chins tilt
skyward. Hands press cool glass. *Bye-bye*, I say.

🌼 Sally Houtman

*N*o matter how old you get, Daughter,
I will always think of you as my child
and love you as much as ever.

❀ Barbara Cage

*Y*ou are such a gift to my life.
You are beautiful, intelligent,
generous, helpful, and kind —
a shining star in my eyes.
Your sparkling personality lights up a room,
and when you are near, spirits are lifted.
It is said that we all need a little joy
every day of our lives.
Well, with the gift of you,
I have a lot of joy every single minute.
With you, I have a beautiful, special
    daughter and friend
who brings so many blessings to my heart.

❀ Jacqueline Schiff

First Lesson

Lie back, daughter, let your head
be tipped back in the cup of my hand.
Gently, and I will hold you. Spread
your arms wide, lie out on the stream
and look high at the gulls. A dead-
man's-float is face down. You will dive
and swim soon enough where this tidewater
ebbs to the sea. Daughter, believe
me, when you tire on the long thrash
to your island, lie up, and survive.
As you float now, where I held you
and let go, remember when fear
cramps your heart what I told you:
lie gently and wide to the light-year
stars, lie back, and the sea will hold you.

❀ Philip Booth

*Y*ou may not control all the events that happen to you, but you can decide not to be reduced by them. Try to be a rainbow in someone's cloud. Do not complain. Make every effort to change things you do not like. If you cannot make a change, change the way you have been thinking. You might find a new solution.

✿ Maya Angelou

*B*e strong about what you believe in. Be firm about who you really are — plus and minus. Know what you will and won't do to get ahead. Know what you can and cannot live with.... You have to take the time to stop and have a conversation with yourself.

✿ Maria Shriver

Mothers and Daughters
Share a Special Love

*T*he mother-daughter relationship is
comprised of a very deep understanding
of and support for each other, and it is
based on an enormous amount of emotion
and love. There is no other relationship
in the world where two women are so
much like one.

❀ Susan Polis Schutz

*F*rom the time I was pregnant with [my
daughter], the love I have felt for her has
transformed and empowered me. It has
fostered empathy, selflessness, compassion,
and courage; it has infused me with a sense
of meaning and purposefulness. Gifted with
love for [her], I have been able to accomplish
tasks, have feelings, and grow in ways I
never dreamed were possible.

❀ Evelyn Bassoff, PhD

*S*he's one of my best friends — she's funny, talented, smart, and kind. Beautiful inside and out, she's a generous, supportive, and sweet person. Her smile and personality can light up a room. We tell each other our secrets, make each other laugh, and have our share of fights. We grew up together. And she's my daughter.

❁ Bethany M. Allen

*D*aughter, darling,
I love you.
I know I don't always understand.
My mother didn't always understand me.
That's the way it is with mothers
and daughters.
But I love you. I will always love you.

❁ Madeleine L'Engle

My Letter to (unnamed)

*T*his is a love letter saying what I am never allowed to say directly to a twelve-year-old daughter of someone whom I am not allowed to name. It is a celebration of who you are right now, and I have to write it obliquely because if I said it to you directly you would say "Ew!" and leave the room in a dramatic huff....

I love that you have started to look appalled and not let me go out the door until you have edited my clothes and it is really kind of great that you are almost always right, even when it means I have to completely change everything I am wearing....

I love that every Monday you become a vegetarian because you are starting to wrestle with ethical dilemmas, and I love that by Thursday you are eating corn dogs from the street fair, but you still love animals and are still figuring it out.

I love that you stick up for kids at school when they are ostracized....

I love that when I make you laugh you have the same crazy smile you did when you were four months old sitting in the baby seat in the back of the car holding your foot straight out in the air with your tiny fist.

I love that you would have no idea how to hide your opinions and your intelligence if you had to....

I love that it never occurs to you to be in anybody's shadow.

I wish you the strengths you have now forever and that they will not be eclipsed but simply join all your strengths for the future, too.

I promise to embarrass you for the rest of your life.

Yours, (not telling).

Naomi Wolf

What a Remarkable Person You Are

There are so many times
when I am in awe of you.

And I want you to know
that I admire you so much!

I admire
the life that you lead and
the kindness that is such a
sweet and natural part of you.

I admire
the way you treat other people.

I admire
how easily a smile finds its way
to your face.

I admire
the work that you do and the
places your journeys take you.

I admire
your dedication to all the right
things and your devotion to your
friends and your family.

I admire
how completely you care and how
willingly you are always there
for the people who need you.

I admire
so many things about you,
and I thank you with all my heart
for being the light that you are...
to my life.

❀ L. N. Mallory

Father and Daughter

I believe the light that shines on you
Will shine on you forever
And though I can't guarantee
There's nothing scary hiding under your bed
I'm gonna stand guard
Like a postcard of a golden retriever
And never leave till I leave you
With a sweet dream in your head

I'm gonna watch you shine
Gonna watch you grow
Gonna paint a sign
So you'll always know
As long as one and one is two
There could never be a father
That loved his daughter more than I love you

🌸 Paul Simon

When I was a young man, I thought life was all about me — about how I'd make my way in the world, become successful, and get the things I want. But then the two of you [my daughters] came into my world with all your curiosity and mischief and those smiles that never fail to fill my heart and light up my day. And suddenly, all my big plans for myself didn't seem so important anymore. I soon found that the greatest joy in my life was the joy I saw in yours.

❀ Barack Obama

There's something like a line of gold thread running through a man's words when he talks to his daughter, and gradually over the years it gets to be long enough for you to pick up in your hands and weave into a cloth that feels like love itself.

❀ John Gregory Brown

Father's Song

Yesterday, against admonishment,
my daughter balanced on the couch back,
fell and cut her mouth.

Because I saw it happen I knew
she was not hurt, and yet
a child's blood's so red
it stops a father's heart.

My daughter cried her tears;
I held some ice
against her lip.
That was the end of it.

Round and round; bow and kiss.
I try to teach her caution;
she tries to teach me risk.

❀ Gregory Orr

"*I have* to save these eight hundred and fifty finger paintings," I once told a friend, who was wondering why there was no room in my garage for my car. "Not just for sentimental value, but also because my four daughters happen to be geniuses. No one has smeared like that since the Renaissance."

❀ Bill Cosby

*T*he father of a daughter is nothing but a high-class hostage. A father turns a stony face to his sons, berates them, shakes his antlers, paws the ground, snorts, runs them off into the underbrush, but when his daughter puts her arm over his shoulder and says, "Daddy, I need to ask you something," he is a pat of butter in a hot frying pan.

❀ Garrison Keillor

In My Daughter's Eyes

In my daughter's eyes
I am a hero
I am strong and wise and I know no fear
But the truth is plain to see
She was sent to rescue me
I see who I want to be
In my daughter's eyes

In my daughter's eyes
Everyone is equal
Darkness turns to light
And the world is at peace
This miracle God gave to me
Gives me strength when I am weak
I find reason to believe
In my daughter's eyes

When she wraps her hand around my finger
Oh, it puts a smile in my heart
Everything becomes a little clearer
I realize what love is all about
It's hangin' on when your heart has had enough
It's giving more when you feel like giving up
I've seen the light
It's in my daughter's eyes

In my daughter's eyes
I can see the future
A reflection of who I am and what will be
Though she'll grow and someday leave
Maybe raise a family
When I'm gone I hope you'll see
How happy she made me
For I'll be there
In my daughter's eyes

🌼 James Slater

Through my daughter's eyes I learned
how to love, smile from within, and live
a happy life. Her eyes told me every day
that even if no one else in this world ever
needed me, she always would. She could
look into my eyes and assure me that we
would grow together and become best
friends, and that's just what we did.

🌼 Debra Heintz Cavataio

When I Look at You, Daughter...

I see someone who has the courage and strength to overcome many obstacles. No matter how many times you fall, you get up again. Even when you want to give up, you don't.

I see someone who has a big heart. You make everyone around you feel loved. You touch so many lives without even knowing it.

In my eyes, I see someone who has been blessed with not only outer beauty but inner beauty. This is the kind of beauty that is everlasting. Time can never take that away from you.

If I could give you only one thing, it would be something I couldn't find in any store and money could never buy. I would give you my eyes, so you could finally see who you really are.

❀ Mary Adisano

When I look at you,
I see a gorgeous butterfly
    emerging from her cocoon,
Someone who is growing and changing,
Becoming more beautiful each and every day.
I see a young woman who is ready
To take on the world and
Whatever it throws her way.
Where there was once a child,
There is now an adult,
Someone who stands up for herself
And for those she loves,
Someone who offers
A helpful hand,
A shoulder to cry on,
And a kind word when she knows
    someone is down.

When I look at you, Daughter,
I see an angel here on earth.

❀ Shannon Koehler

What I Want for You, Daughter

I want you to be proud of yourself for being a good person. What matters isn't the awards you receive, but the way you treat other people. I want you to do the things you have a passion for — not just those that are most popular.

I want you to be proud of your heritage. Choose to live your life in ways that honor your ancestors. Those who paved the way for you have passed on the torch to you. Carry it with dignity and responsibility.

I want you to always be a woman of action. Dreams are important, but only acting on them will make them happen. I want you to find peace within yourself. Peace may not always be in the world, but it is always deep inside you.

I want you to be happy in a natural way. I want to see your smiles, hear your laughter, and watch the spring in your step. Seek happiness, and good things will follow.

I want you to surround yourself with good friends who want only the best for you and who stick with you at all times, celebrating your successes and empathizing with your setbacks.

I want you to know the strength and abundance of my love. Close your eyes for a moment and feel my love wrapped around you. Feel it surrounding you wherever you go. Let my love bring you friendship, the comfort of my arms, and the confidence of my faith in your capabilities.

I want you to always know I'm thinking of you with love, pride, and the highest admiration for the beautiful woman you've become.

Jacqueline Schiff

Remember
Who You Are

Don't ever lose sight of the gift that is you. When life seems to knock you down, get back up and get back in the game. Remember what you're made of. Remember what's flowing in your veins. Remember what you were given, and remember what you went out and created on your own. Like any great masterpiece, you're not done yet. Inside you is the best of everyone who has come before you — and the best of everyone yet to be. You can forget some of what life hands you, but never, ever forget who you are.

❀ Rachel Snyder

This life is yours
Take the power
to choose what you want to do
and do it well
Take the power
to love what you want in life
and love it honestly
Take the power
to make your life
healthy
exciting
worthwhile
and very happy

❀ Susan Polis Schutz

You have so much to offer,
so much to give,
and so much you deserve
to receive in return.
Don't ever doubt that.

❀ Janet A. Sullivan

To My Daughter, with Love, on the Important Things in Life

A mother tries to provide her daughter with insight
into the important things in life
in order to make her life
as happy and fulfilling as possible

A mother tries to teach her daughter
to be good, always helpful to other people
to be fair, always treating others equally
to have a positive attitude at all times
to always make things right when they are wrong
to know herself well
to know what her talents are
to set goals for herself
to not be afraid of working too hard to reach her goals

A mother tries to teach her daughter
to have many interests to pursue
to laugh and have fun every day
to appreciate the beauty of nature
to enter into friendships with good people
to honor their friendships and always be a true friend
to appreciate the importance of the family
and to particularly respect and love our elder members
to use her intelligence at all times
to listen to her emotions
to adhere to her values

A mother tries to teach her daughter
to not be afraid to stick to her beliefs
to not follow the majority when the majority
    is wrong
to carefully plan a life for herself
to vigorously follow her chosen path
to enter into a relationship with someone
    worthy of herself
to love this person unconditionally
    with her body and mind
to share all that she has learned in life with
    this person

If I have provided you with an insight
into most of these things
then I have succeeded as a mother
in what I hoped to accomplish in raising you
If many of these things slipped by
while we were all so busy
I have a feeling that you know them anyway
One thing I am sure of, though
I have taught you to be proud of the fact
that you are a woman equal to all men and
I have loved you every second of your life
I have supported you at all times
and as a mother, as a person, and as a friend
I will always continue to cherish and love
everything about you
my beautiful daughter

❀ Susan Polis Schutz

This Work of Art Called "Your Life" Is the Greatest Gift of All

*E*ach day is like a blank canvas waiting for you to paint the picture. If you have no idea where to start, just start painting — anywhere for now will do. You'll get your direction. You've got to stir up the gift inside you so it will know you're serious; then it will take you someplace you've never been.

Life is beautiful, and most things will turn out right. It may get messy sometimes when there are storms, failures, and disappointments, but you will survive. You can't plan every move. You can't control everything. There will be surprises. Just trust that there's a bigger plan.

When you come up with bright ideas, follow through on them. Don't worry if you have to learn the same old lesson over and over — we all do that. That's life, too, but it's just one section on the canvas. Depending on how you look at all the lessons you've learned from your perceived mistakes, the whole picture can be a masterpiece.

Don't be too goal-oriented or base your happiness on conditions. Don't ever put off being happy, even if your dreams never come true or if you never get stuff right. Dreams are important, but you are more than your dreams. Life is the prize. Always count even the tiniest blessings, and be happy no matter what.

❀ Donna Fargo

Helping My Daughter Move into Her First Apartment

This is all I am to her now:
a pair of legs in running shoes,

two arms strung with braided wire.
She heaves a carton sagging with CDs

at me and I accept it gladly, lifting
with my legs, not bending over,

raising each foot high enough
to clear the step. Fortunate to be

of any use to her at all,
I wrestle, stooped and single-handed,

with her mattress in the stairwell,
saying nothing as it pins me,

sweating, to the wall. Vacuum cleaner,
spiny cactus, five-pound sacks

of rice and lentils slumped
against my heart: up one flight

of stairs and then another,
down again with nothing in my arms

❀ Sue Ellen Thompson

I remember when
you were so tiny
I could cradle you in my arms
and watch you sleep.
When you awoke,
you'd smile at me
and curl all your fingers
around one of mine
and hold on so very tightly
I thought you'd never let go.
Those same precious fingers
wound themselves
around my heart, too...
and to this day,
they have never let go.

❁ Maria Rachel Hooley

The World Needs You Now

The world needs you now —
more than you know,
more than you can imagine.

The world needs your gifts:
your heart,
your compassion,
your understanding,
your ability to listen, to speak,
to feel, to act...
the gifts that only you can give,
in the way that you and you alone
can give them.

The world needs you,
and the world needs you now —
more than you know,
more than you can ever imagine.

✿ Rachel Snyder

Know Your Power

*A*s long as we recognize the power within us, we will continue to have choices, and we will continue to lead.

The source of that power can be the other people who guide us. It can come from the knowledge that courageous women throughout history paved the way for us. It can come from our roots and our families, which give us strength. And it must come from within ourselves — from our faith, our accomplishments, and our values.

Know your power.

When you do, others will know your power, too.

❀ Nancy Pelosi

Don't Ever Stop Reaching and Growing

*D*on't be afraid of growing, changing, or living your life. No matter where you go or what you do, the true joy of life lies in the journey — not the destination. Search for your purpose, seek out your passions, and do what you love. It's not how long you live, but how you choose to live the days you are given, so choose to make the most of every opportunity you receive. Follow your dreams wherever they may lead, and live all the days of your life.

❀ Julie Anne Ford

*L*ean against a tree
and dream your world of dreams
Work hard at what you like to do
and try to overcome all obstacles
Laugh at your mistakes
and praise yourself for learning from them
Pick some flowers
and appreciate the beauty of nature
Be honest with people
and enjoy the good in them
Don't be afraid to show your emotions
Laughing and crying make you feel better
Love your friends and family
   with your entire being
They are the most important part of your life
Feel the calmness on a quiet sunny day
and plan what you want to accomplish in life
Find a rainbow
and live your world of dreams

❀ Susan Polis Schutz

I Have So Many Wishes for You

I want the world for you, but much more than that — and I don't care if it's a cliché — I want you to be happy. If I had magic powers I'd wish on you the ability to take pleasure in small things — a swim in the sea, a good book read on a rug in a summer garden, a delicious meal shared with friends. I say this because when I was 21 I wrote in my diary: "What am I going to do!!! Nothing's happening. What if it never does?" I laughed, even a few years later when I came across this entry, but what I regret most about my panicked 21-year-old self is that I forgot to live in the present. I was so concerned with the future and my place in it that I forgot to luxuriate in being young.

❀ Esther Freud

*M*y greatest wish is for my daughters to discover their passion, whatever it is.

❀ Arianna Huffington

I wish you courage... to handle those days that, for whatever reason, seem more complicated and harder to get through.

I wish you hope... that you'll always realize there is a rainbow waiting at the end of every tunnel.

❀ Betsy Bertram

I wish you love — to shine like blue skies above you wherever you go, so you always know you're in the hearts of so many people.

❀ Jacqueline Schiff

*M*y dreams for your life might not always be the same ones you seek. But one thing remains the same: your happiness will always be my greatest treasure.

❀ Nancy Gilliam

You've Done a Beautiful Job of Growing Up

I don't have to close my eyes to imagine you when you were a cuddly, soft, delightful baby. I don't have to search through photo albums to remember you — the child who had a special place in my arms, my life, and my heart. All I have to do is look into your beautiful eyes. Each time I do, your life parades across my memories, tugs at my heartstrings, and brings me back to days that were so special.

It's hard to accept those times are gone and you're all grown up. Yet I still love what I see when I look into your eyes. I see a deep love for others, especially family. I see loyalty, determination, goals, and dreams. I see a young adult who has faced life's challenges and temptations and made the best of them. I see dreams that have come true and dreams you've had to give up on. I see the results of those years, and I am proud of who you have become.

My own heart has been changed many times by yours. It has filled with compassion when you were sad or hurt. It has overflowed with gratitude and joy when you have reached out to me, and others, in affection and kindness. It has grown in knowledge and understanding when you opened my eyes to a new way of looking at something or stood your ground when I was wrong. Your heart will always be connected to mine. There's no distance too far, no person, no circumstance, no amount of time that will ever be able to come between us.

This love I have for you has been growing a very long time. With excitement and expectation I look to the future, knowing I will get to share much of it with you. I want you to remember that no matter where we are on this road of life, every path we take will always lead us back... to each other.

Barbara Cage

I'm So Proud of You

You've brought immense joy to my life, making me proud in countless ways. You always know how to make me smile or laugh — something you've been able to do since you were a little girl.

I adore talking with you and sharing in the enthusiasm and excitement of new things going on in your life.

It warms my heart to know how fortunate I've been to experience the joy that comes with having a daughter like you.

❀ Debbie Burton-Peddle

I am more proud of my daughter than I can possibly express. She is a beautiful, delightful, funny woman. She marches to her own drummer. It may not be my music, but I guess, in a way, I marched to my own drummer and it wasn't necessarily [her] music.

❀ Barbara Walters

*Y*ou are such a beautiful and profound part of my life. I am so proud of the person you are and the wonderful difference you have made and make to me, our family, and this world. You are beautiful inside and out. There is no one else like you. You are truly one of a kind. I not only love you with all my heart, but I genuinely like you, and I'm so glad you're my daughter.

❀ Deborah Correia McDaniels

Wherever You Go,
Daughter...

*A*lways remember that —
separately or together —
home is in our hearts
and the love we have
for each other.
It is in our daily prayers
for safety, health, and strength.
It is in our search for peace
amidst life's struggles
and in our pursuit of dreams,
knowledge, and happiness.
It's in the safe haven
of the bond between us.

Home will always be
in our hearts
and in the love we share.

❀ Linda Sackett-Morrison

...My Love Goes with You

You are such a delight
such a joy
such a beautiful person
The love I see in your eyes for me
is so moving and rewarding
And I hope you see and feel
the infinite love I have for you
Whatever you do
wherever you go
always know that
I am always here
in every way
for you
I love you
— Susan Polis Schutz

Acknowledgments continued...

We gratefully acknowledge the permission granted by the following authors, publishers, and authors' representatives to reprint poems or excerpts from their publications: *Literary Mama*, www.literarymama.com, for "My Daughter in the Garden" by Sally Houtman (*Literary Mama*: December 6, 2009). Copyright © 2009 by Sally Houtman. All rights reserved. Viking Penguin, a division of Penguin Group (USA), Inc., for "First Lesson" from LIFELINES by Philip Booth. Copyright © 1999 by Philip Booth. All rights reserved. Random House, Inc. and Little, Brown Book Group for "You may not control all the events..." from LETTER TO MY DAUGHTER by Maya Angelou. Copyright © 2008 by Maya Angelou. All rights reserved. Grand Central Publishing for "Be strong about what you believe in" from TEN THINGS I WISH I'D KNOWN BEFORE I WENT OUT INTO THE REAL WORLD by Maria Shriver. Copyright © 2000 by Maria Shriver. Reprinted by permission of Grand Central Publishing. All rights reserved. Dutton, a division of Penguin Group (USA), Inc., for "From the time I was pregnant..." from CHERISHING OUR DAUGHTERS by Evelyn Bassoff, PhD. Copyright © 1998 by Evelyn Bassoff. All rights reserved. Bethany M. Allen for "She's one of my best friends..." from "My Girl" from RISE UP SINGING, edited by Cecelie S. Berry. Copyright © 2003 by Bethany M. Allen. All rights reserved. Random House Value Publishing, a division of Random House, Inc., for "Daughter, darling I love you" from MOTHERS & DAUGHTERS by Madeleine L'Engle. Copyright © 1997 by Crosswicks, Ltd. All rights reserved. Paul Simon Music for "Father and Daughter" by Paul Simon. Copyright © 2006 by Paul Simon Music. All rights reserved. Houghton Mifflin Harcourt Publishing Company for "There's something like a line of gold thread..." from DECORATIONS IN A RUINED CEMETERY by John Gregory Brown. Copyright © 1994 by John Gregory Brown. Reprinted by permission. All rights reserved. University of Pittsburgh Press for "Father's Song" from CITY OF SALT by Gregory Orr. Copyright © 1995 by Gregory Orr. All rights reserved. Doubleday, a division of Random House, Inc., for "'I *have* to save these...'" from TIME FLIES by Bill Cosby. Copyright © 1987 by William H. Cosby, Jr. All rights reserved. Prairie Home Productions, LLC, for "The father of a daughter..." from THE BOOK OF GUYS by Garrison Keillor. Copyright © 1993 by Garrison Keillor. All rights reserved. Chrysalis Music for "In My Daughter's Eyes" by James Slater. Copyright © 2006 by James Slater. All rights reserved. Rachel Snyder for "Remember Who You Are" and "The World Needs You Now." Copyright © 2008, 2010 by Rachel Snyder. All rights reserved. PrimaDonna Entertainment Corp. for "This Work of Art Called 'Your Life'..." by Donna Fargo. Copyright © 2010 by PrimaDonna Entertainment Corp. All rights reserved. Autumn House Press for "Helping My Daughter Move into Her First Apartment" from THE GOLDEN HOUR by Sue Ellen Thompson. Copyright © 2006 by Sue Ellen Thompson. All rights reserved. Anchor Books, a division of Random House, Inc., for "As long as we recognize the power..." from KNOW YOUR POWER: A MESSAGE TO AMERICA'S DAUGHTERS by Nancy Pelosi. Copyright © 2008 by Nancy Pelosi. All rights reserved. Julie Anne Ford for "Don't be afraid of growing...." Copyright © 2010 by Julie Anne Ford. All rights reserved. Esther Freud for "I want the world for you..." from "Letter to My Daughter" (*The Times*: March 21, 2009). Copyright © 2009 by Esther Freud. All rights reserved. *Newsweek* for "My greatest wish is for my daughters..." by Arianna Huffington from "My Journey to the Top" (*Newsweek*: October 15, 2007). Copyright © 2007 by Newsweek, Inc. All rights reserved. Used by permission and protected by the Copyright Laws of the United States. Barbara Cage for "You've Done a Beautiful Job of Growing Up." Copyright © 2010 by Barbara Cage. All rights reserved. Debbie Burton-Peddle for "You've brought immense joy to my life...." Copyright © 2010 by Debbie Burton-Peddle. All rights reserved. Vintage Books, a division of Random House, Inc., for "I am more proud of my daughter..." from AUDITION: A MEMOIR by Barbara Walters. Copyright © 2008, 2009 by Barbara Walters. All rights reserved. Deborah Correia McDaniels for "You are such a beautiful and profound part of my life." Copyright © 2010 by Deborah Correia McDaniels. All rights reserved. Linda Sackett-Morrison for "Always remember that...." Copyright © 2010 by Linda Sackett-Morrison. All rights reserved.

A careful effort has been made to trace the ownership of selections used in this anthology in order to obtain permission to reprint copyrighted material and give proper credit to the copyright owners. If any error or omission has occurred, it is completely inadvertent, and we would like to make corrections in future editions provided that written notification is made to the publisher:

BLUE MOUNTAIN ARTS, INC., P.O. Box 4549, Boulder, Colorado 80306.